Chin
Vegetarian
Cooking

Daniel Reid

PERIPLUS

Introduction

Many people turn to vegetarian diets for reasons of health, only to switch back to meat diets for reasons of taste, or because they fail to obtain adequate nutrition from vegetarian food. In modern Western diets, vegetarian food is usually regarded as a stark, not-so-healthy regimen devoid of culinary pleasure and nutritional power, and vegetarian cooking has therefore never achieved the gourmet heights of conventional meat-based cookery in the Western world.

In Chinese cuisine, however, vegetarian cooking has always been an important branch of the classical culinary arts, and like all Chinese cooking, equal emphasis is always placed on considerations of health as well as flavour. Furthermore, due to the Chinese genius for rendering soy bean products into all sorts of creative, tasty substitutes for meat, eggs and dairy products, Chinese vegetarian diets provide even more well balanced, high quality nutrition, including protein, than conventional diets based on animal products.

Many of these methods of cooking were developed over many centuries in the vegetarian kitchens of Buddhist monasteries in China. Highly nutritious, easy to digest, and always delicious, Chinese vegetarian cuisine is a serious, worthy alternative to any meat-based diet, and it may be as easily prepared at home as any homestyle Chinese dish.

The recipes in this book may be used to prepare complete, well balanced vegetarian meals for a table of all-vegetarian diners, or you may simply select one or two dishes to prepare for a vegetarian guest at a meal in which meat dishes are prepared for other guests at the same table. One of the advantages of Chinese vegetarian cooking is that you can easily prepare a nutritionally complete meal in a single dish, using a combination of tofu and various vegetables, for just one person who is strictly vegetarian, while preparing meat and seafood dishes for others at the same meal.

Another way to use these recipes is to declare one or two 'veggie nights' at your own table each week, and prepare meals that are entirely vegetarian. This is a good way to gradually reduce the meat and other animal products in your diet, without giving them up altogether, while at the same time growing accustomed to the delicious taste and healthy benefits of Chinese vegetarian food.

Glossary

Oyster sauce: A Cantonese speciality, regular oyster sauce is a very flavoursome soy-based sauce with oyster extract. Vegetarians should look for the vegetarian version which is sometimes sold as 'mushroom oyster sauce'.

Red dates: Also known as Chinese jujube, or *hong zao* in Mandarin, Chinese red dates is the size of a round olive and although sour when raw, it is sweet when matured and dried. Red dates are often eaten during Chinese New Year.

Sichuan pepper: Also known as flower pepper or fagara, this spice has a sharp pungence that tingles and slightly numbs the lips and tongue, an effect known in Chinese as *ma la* ('numb hot'). To make Sichuan pepper-salt powder, dry-toast Sichuan peppercorns with sea salt (2 tablespoons peppercorns to 1/2 teaspoon salt), grind to a fine powder and sprinkle over cooked dishes as garnish.

Sesame paste: Not to be confused with sweet sesame paste made from black sesame seeds which is used in some snacks and desserts, savoury sesame paste is made from ground, roasted sesame seeds and comes in glass jars covered with oil. It is quite hard and needs to be mixed with a little sesame oil or water to make it into a smooth paste. If you can't find it, use Middle Eastern tahini mixed with sesame oil to give it a more pronounced flavour.

Tiger lily buds: The dried, unopened buds of the tiger lily are also known as golden needles and are readily available from Chinese stores. Soak in warm water before cooking and discard the hard ends.

White fungus: Also known as white wood ears, white fungus has a crunchy texture and a slightly sweet flavour.

Wine: Wine is used frequently in Chinese cooking as a tenderizer, to eliminate rank tastes in meat and fish, to blend flavours and to enhance taste.

Wood ear fungus: Also known as dried black fungus, tree ears or cloud ears, wood ear fungus is dull black whren dried but becomes shiny black after soaking. Readily available from Chinese stores.

Brown Rice with Stir-fried Diced Vegetables

This is a tasty and convenient 'one-dish meal' that's packed full of various flavours and textures to satisfy the palate, while providing the full range of nutritional building blocks for health. Many of the ingredients, such as *shiitake* and seaweed, have potent medicinal properties. For large families, this is an excellent way to feed many mouths a healthy meal with minimum fuss in the kitchen.

220 g (1 cup) brown rice
2 15-cm (6-in) strips dried *konbu* seaweed, soaked in 625 ml (2 1/2 cups) cool water, 20 minutes
2 tablespoons oil
2 medium yellow or white onions, cubed
4 cloves garlic, finely chopped
1 medium carrot, peeled, halved lengthways then sliced thinly
1 medium green capsicum (bell pepper), cleaned and diced into 1-cm (1/2-in) squares
6 large dried *shiitake* mushrooms, soaked in hot water, diced small
80 g (1/2 cup) fresh or frozen green peas
Fresh coriander (cilantro) leaves, to garnish

Seasonings
1/2 teaspoon salt
1 teaspoon sugar
2 teaspoon soy sauce
1 teaspoon ground black pepper

1 Wash rice thoroughly in several changes of water until the water runs clear. In a bowl soak the rice with enough water to cover by 2 1/2 cm (1 in), and set aside to soak for several hours, preferably overnight. Just before cooking, drain the rice.

2 Slice *konbu* into 1-cm (1/2-in) strips and return to its soaking liquid. Using a small saucepan, boil the *konbu*, then lower heat and simmer to reduce liquid for about 20 minutes. Set aside.

3 Place drained rice, *konbu* and *konbu* broth in a pan, bring to a boil and simmer until done, about 20 to 25 minutes. Cool rice and set aside *konbu*.

4 Heat 2 tablespoons oil in wok or roomy pan until hot, then add onion and garlic. Stir-fry for 1 minute then add the carrots, capsicum, *shiitake*, seasonings and, finally, the peas. Continue to stir-fry for 2 to 3 minutes, then add the cooked rice and *konbu*. Mix well and cook until rice is heated through, about 5 minutes.

5 Adjust seasoning. Turn off heat, and transfer rice and vegetables to a serving bowl.

If you don't like the taste of konbu seaweed, or if you don't have any on hand, or if you are simply in a hurry in the kitchen, you may substitute any kind of vegetable soup stock for the konbu broth. You may also experiment with other combinations of vegetables, such as fresh corn, white turnip, and other types of mushroom. Diners may wish to add a dab of good chilli sauce to their portions.

Serves 4
Preparation time: **20 mins + overnight soaking**
Cooking time: **1 hour**

Chinese Rice and Soy Beans

Soy beans have always formed the backbone of the Chinese vegetarian diet by providing abundant sources of high quality vegetable protein and oil, especially advantageous since it contains virtually no cholesterol. Brown rice is regarded as a perfectly balanced food in terms of the 'five elements' (earth, wood, metal, fire and water) and in combination with soy beans provides all the essential amino acids required for protein synthesis in the human body. It is also a rich source of B vitamins, minerals and fibre. This dish is meant to be served as the rice dish in a meal, and may be combined with any type of Chinese food.

220 g (1 cup) brown rice
500 ml (2 cups) water
100 g (1/2) cup soy beans
750 ml (3 cups) water
1/2 teaspoon salt

Garnishes
1 bunch fresh coriander (cilantro) leaves, finely chopped
2 spring onions (scallions), finely chopped
1 medium carrot, peeled, diced and blanched for 2–3 minutes
1 small red and green capsicum (bell pepper), finely chopped
Ground black (or Sichuan) pepper to taste

1 Wash rice in several changes of water until water runs clear, then place in a medium-sized cooking pot with 500 ml (2 cups) water. Cover and leave to soak overnight.
2 Pick over soy beans for grit, then wash the soy beans well. Drain, then place in a separate medium-sized cooking pot with enough water to cover by at least 2 1/2 cm (1 in). Cover and leave to soak overnight.
3 Next day, drain excess water from soy beans and discard. Add 750 ml (3 cups) fresh water to the pot of beans and bring to the boil. Cover, then lower heat and simmer slowly until all the water has been absorbed, about 1 1/2 hours. Check the beans occasionally to make sure they don't scorch. When beans are soft, transfer them to a bowl and set aside to cool.
4 Add the salt to the soaked rice and water in the pot (do not discard the water), and bring to a full boil. Cover tightly, reduce heat to very low, and simmer slowly for about 30 minutes. Do not remove lid while cooking. It's done when you hear the rice crackling on the bottom of the pot. Turn off the heat and let the pot rest, covered, for 15 minutes, then transfer to a bowl and set aside to cool, turning the rice once or twice with a spoon to cool and dry evenly.
5 When rice and beans have cooled but are still warm, carefully fold them together in a large serving bowl. Stir in all or any of the garnishes and serve. You may also use this rice-and-beans combo as the basis of fried rice dishes.

Serves 4
Preparation time: overnight soaking
Cooking time: 50 mins

Chinese Vegetarian Sandwich with Sesame Sauce

This is a convenient, modern adaptation of a sort of 'Chinese sandwich' that is traditionally made with flat wholemeal bread which requires special ovens and a lot of experience to prepare properly. Instead, we substitute any heavy, high quality wholegrain bakery bread, thinly sliced and toasted, and this provides equally good, if not better, results. The key to any good sandwich, besides fresh ingredients, is the spread, and in Chinese sandwiches sesame paste is the key to the spread.

3 thin slices of heavy wholegrain bread, toasted

1 medium tomato, thinly sliced

12–15 fresh celery leaves, coarsely chopped

2–3 leaves fresh iceberg lettuce, torn into bite-sized pieces

1 small onion, thinly sliced

Spread

35 g (1/4 cup) raw sunflower seeds, presoaked at least 3 hours (or overnight) in cool water and drained

2 tablespoons dark Chinese sesame paste (or tahini) blended with 3 teaspoons water

1 tablespoon sesame oil

1/4 teaspoon salt

1/2 teaspoon sugar

1 teaspoon soy sauce

1 teaspoon ground black pepper

1 To prepare the spread, place all the ingredients in a blender, and blend to a smooth paste. Taste and adjust salt if necessary.

2 To assemble the sandwich, slice and toast the bread. Place a slice of toast on a plate and cover with one-quarter of the spread. Arrange half the tomato, chopped celery leaves, lettuce and onions on top of the spread. Top with a second slice of toast spread-side down, then cover the top of that slice with spread and arrange remaining vegetables on it. Complete the sandwich with the third slice of toast placed spread-side down.

3 Cut in half with sharp knife, or serve whole.

As with all sandwiches, you may improvise and experiment with a variety of different fillings, as well as different types of wholemeal toast (sourdough rye is especially good with the Chinese sesame spread).
As long as you use the basic sesame sauce, or some version of it, as your spread, the sandwich will taste 'Chinese'. It will also have the unique health virtues of Chinese food, for sesame paste is a very potent source of nutritional elements.

Serves 1
Preparation time: **10 mins**
Assembling time: **5 mins**

Poached Vegetable Salad with Sesame Oil Dressing

Poaching is an excellent way to cook almost any type of vegetable for Chinese salads. Poaching preserves colour, nutrients, taste and texture, while briefly cooking the vegetable to just the right point. Creative improvisation may be applied in selecting the vegetables and mixing the dressings. In Chinese dressings, dark sesame oil plays the role taken by olive oil in European salad dressings; the rest is up to your imagination and taste buds.

250 g (8 oz) fresh lotus roots, washed and drained
200 g (6 1/2 oz) long green beans, tops and tails removed, halved
2 large stalks celery, stringy fibre removed, sliced
1 medium carrot, peeled and sliced
80 g (1/2 cup) fresh or frozen green peas

Dressing
3 tablespoons mushroom oyster sauce (*su hao yio*)
2 cloves garlic, finely minced
1 teaspoon sesame oil;
2 teaspoons dark sesame paste (or tahini)
1/2 teaspoon salt

1 Place lotus roots in pot, cover with 2 litres (8 cups) water and bring to a full boil. Cover, lower heat, and simmer for 40 minutes. Remove, rinse in cool water, and set aside to cool; reserve the lotus root stock for blanching the greens. When cool, cut lotus roots into round slices about 1/2 cm (1/4 in) thick.

2 Add the beans to the boiling lotus root stock, let the water return to boil, then remove beans from water with slotted spoon as soon as they turn shiny dark green; place in colander, rinse in cool water, and set aside.

3 Bring a fresh pan of water to the boil with 1 teaspoon salt added. Add the carrots and cook for 3 minutes; remove with slotted spoon, rinse in cool water, and set aside to drain. Add the peas, then remove with slotted spoon after 1 minute; rinse and set aside.

4 In a large salad bowl, stir to combine the dressing ingredients, then add all the vegetables and toss together until well mixed.

5 Transfer to a smaller salad bowl or platter and serve.

Lotus roots are seasonal and not always available, so you may use other ingredients, such as poached broccoli, potato and cauliflower. For those who like to spice up their salads, set the table with some ground black pepper, Sichuan peppercorn-salt powder, and some dried chilli flakes. Chopped parsley or fresh coriander (cilantro) leaves also goes well on this salad.

Serves 4
Preparation time: **30 mins**
Cooking time: **50 mins**

Shredded Steamed Pumpkin Salad with Chinese Vinaigrette Dressing

Pumpkin is one of the most nutritious of all vegetables, easy to digest, and inexpensive. In this recipe, it's combined with green capsicum and bean sheets, and seasoned with a savoury Chinese vinaigrette.

500 g (1 lb) fresh pumkin, peeled, seeds removed and cut into wedges to yield 2 cups
1 piece dried mung bean sheet or 60 g (2 oz) glass noodles
1 green capsicum (bell pepper), thinly sliced
3 teaspoons sesame seeds, dry roasted and roughly pounded
Chilli oil to garnish (optional)

Dressing
2 teaspoons soy sauce
1 teaspoons vinegar
1 teaspoon black pepper
1/2 teaspoon salt
1/2 teaspoon sugar
3 teaspoons sesame oil

1 Set up a steamer and place the peeled wedges of pumpkin on a heatproof plate and set on rack in steamer. Cover tightly and steam for 25 minutes; remove from steamer and let cool, then cut into thin strips 1/2 to 1 cm (1/4 to 1/2 in) thick; set aside.

2 Meanwhile, place the dried bean sheet in a wide shallow bowl, pour boiling water over it to cover completely, and let steep for 30 minutes. Drain off the water and, when cool enough to handle, cut the bean sheet into long thin strips about 1/2 cm (1/4 in) wide. If using glass noodles, soak in hot water for 20 minutes and drain.

3 Stir all dressing ingredients, except the sesame oil, in a small bowl and blend well using a wire whisk or fork; slowly dribble in the sesame oil while beating continuously, until well blended.

4 Place the sliced pumpkin, bean sheet strips, and shredded capsicum in a large salad bowl. Stir the dressing again to blend, then pour evenly over the vegetables, and toss until vegetables are completely coated with the dressing.

5 Transfer to a smaller serving dish, sprinkle with ground sesame seeds, and drizzle with chilli oil, if desired.

Serves 4–6
Preparation time: **40 mins + 20 mins soaking time**
Cooking time: **40 mins**

Poached Eggplant Salad

3 medium eggplants
(aubergines), long
tubular variety (about
500 g or 1 lb)
Fresh coriander (cilantro)
leaves, to garnish
(optional)

Dressing
6 cloves garlic, finely
minced
1 teaspoon soy sauce
2 teaspoos white rice
(or other) vinegar
1/2 teaspoon salt
1 teaspoon sugar
1 teaspoon black pepper
1 tablespoon sesame oil

1 Bring a large pot of water to a full boil, then add the whole eggplants; let water return to the boil, then lower heat and simmer until the eggplants change colour and begin to wilt, about 8 minutes.
2 Remove from water and set in a colander to drain. Cut eggplants in half lengthways, then cut each half into 5-cm (2-in) pieces, and place in a mixing bowl.
3 In a small bowl stir together all dressing ingredients, except sesame oil. Then, using a whisk or fork, add in the sesame oil while beating continuously until the dressing is well blended. Pour the dressing evenly over the eggplant and toss to blend.
4 Transfer to a smaller serving dish.

Serves 4
Preparation time: **5 mins**
Cooking time: **8 mins**

Ladies' Fingers Salad

30 pieces fresh ladies'
fingers (okra), washed
and drained
Fresh basil or Chinese
celery leaf to garnish
(optional)

Dressing
6 cloves garlic, finely
minced
2 slices ginger, finely
minced
1/2 teaspoon salt
1 teaspoon sugar
2 teaspoon vinegar
1 teaspoon soy sauce
2 tablespoons sesame oil

1 To make the dressing: place all ingredients, except
the sesame oil, in a small bowl. Slowly dribble in the
sesame oil while beating continuously with a whisk or
a fork until the dressing is well blended.

2 Bring a large pot of water to a full boil, then add the
ladies' fingers. Return to the boil, cover and lower heat
to medium, and simmer for 3 to 4 minutes, until the
ladies' fingers become shiny dark green. Remove from
water and drain well in a colander.

3 Arrange the cooked ladies' fingers on a serving
platter, then slowly pour the dressing evenly over
them, add garnish if desired, and serve.

Serves 4
Preparation time: **10 mins**
Cooking time: **15 mins**

Spicy Beancurd-skin Rolls

Beancurd skin is the thin rich layer of soy protein that forms on the surface of soy bean milk while it's being boiled to make beancurd. When fresh, it is regarded as the crème-de-la-crème of all soy products. Since this is a highly perishable product, it is only available fresh in traditional Asian markets located near tofu and soy milk producers. The dried variety, however, is available in many Oriental grocers, and while it cannot quite match the flavour and texture of the fresh variety, it has the same nutritional benefits and is easier to work with in the kitchen.

200 g (2 cups) fresh mung bean sprouts
50 g (1/2 cup) *enoki* mushrooms, separated and cleaned
2 medium carrots, peeled and shredded
110 g (1 cup) sugar snaps, sliced length-ways
4 sheets dried beancurd skin
1 tablespoon flour
2 tablespoons oil

Sauce
2 tablespoons dark sesame paste (or tahini) blended with 5 teaspoons water
1/2 teaspoon thick soy sauce
1/2 teaspoon salt
3 1/2 teaspoons sugar
4 teaspoons vinegar
1 teaspoon sesame oil
2 cloves garlic, finely minced
1 spring onion (scallion), finely sliced
2 slices ginger, finely minced
1 fresh red chilli, seeds removed, finely minced

1 Bring a large pot of lightly salted water to the boil then add the bean sprouts, mushrooms, carrot and sugar snaps. Stir a few times, leave in water about 30 seconds, then remove to a colander, rinse in cool water, and set aside to drain.

2 Cut each sheet of beancurd skin in half, then lay one half on top of the other, to make 4 double-layered sheets. The aim is to get rectangles of roughly 20 x 25 cm (8 x 10 in).

3 In a bowl, add flour to vegetables and mix well. Divide the vegetables evenly into 4 portions, and place them neatly on the edge of the 4 double-layered beancurd sheets; roll the sheets over the vegetables to form tubular rolls.

4 In a flat heavy frying pan, heat the oil until hot but not smoking. Place the beancurd skin rolls in the pan and fry about 2 minutes, then turn and fry the other side for about 2 minutes. The skins should turn light golden brown, but be careful not to scorch them.

5 When done, remove from skillet and place on paper towels on a plate to remove excess oil.

6 When cool, cut each roll at an angle into 3 pieces and serve with the dipping sauce.

7 To make the sauce, stir the liquid ingredients in a mixing bowl until well blended, then stir in the minced items. Transfer to a smaller bowl and serve.

Serves 4
Preparation time: **15 mins**
Cooking time: **10 mins**

Crinkle-fried Dried Beancurd

This recipe employs a traditional Sichuan cooking technique called *gan bian* ('crinkle-fry'), whereby the main ingredient is continuously stir-fried in a small amount of oil over medium heat, until it starts to 'crinkle', such as in the famous Sichuan dish, *gan bian si ji dou*, 'crinkle-fried green beans'. Here the method is applied to dried beancurd, which is then combined with carrot and celery leaf to add some crunch and crisp to the crinkle!

3 tablespoons oil
1 teaspoon salt
1 medium carrot, peeled and finely shredded
280 g (9 oz) dried beancurd (*tofu gan*), cut into 1 x 4-cm (1/2 x 1 1/2-in) sticks (about 3 cups)
1 teaspoon vinegar
1 teaspoon sesame oil
1 handful fresh Chinese celery leaves, chopped

Sauce
3 teaspoons sweet hoisin sauce
1 teaspoon sugar
3 teaspoons wine
2 teaspoons soy sauce

1 Heat oil in a wok until hot but not smoking. Add 1 teaspoon salt to the hot oil, then stir in the dried beancurd sticks. Stir-fry continuously on medium heat, until the beancurd starts to crinkle and gets a bit crispy; this usually takes about 10 to 15 minutes; remove with slottted spoon and set aside on a plate.

2 In the remaining oil, add the carrot, stir-fry 30 seconds, then add the sauce ingredients and cook another minute before returning the fried beancurd sticks to the pan. Stir-fry 1 minute, ensuring that beancurd sticks are coated in the sauce, then add vinegar and stir-fry 30 seconds more. Turn off the heat, add sesame oil, and toss to combine.

3 Transfer to a serving plate, garnish evenly with the chopped celery leaf, and serve.

For those who don't care for the taste of Chinese celery leaf, chopped basil or fresh coriander (cilantro) are excellent alternatives.

Serves 4
Preparation time: **10 mins**
Cooking time: **25 mins**

Steamed Tofu with Spiced Shiitake and Wood Ear Fungus

The combination of spiced *shiitake* and wood ears was developed years ago by the author's wife for this recipe—a signature dish in her restaurant in Taipei, Taiwan. It may be applied to many different types of dishes, including noodles and dumplings, and as a filling for crêpes or beancurd skin rolls. Here this delicious and highly fortifying blend is used to spice up and balance the otherwise neutral tofu.

1 cake soft tofu (300 g or 10 oz)

5 dried *shiitake* mushrooms, soaked in hot water for 20 minutes, stalk removed and finely diced

3 pieces wood ear fungus, finely diced (if using dried wood ears, soak in hot water for 20 minutes)

5 cloves garlic, finely minced

5 slices ginger, finely minced

6 spring onions (scallions), finely minced

Fresh coriander (cilantro), chopped, to garnish

Seasoning
1 teaspoon salt
1 teaspoon sugar
1 teaspoon soy sauce
1 tablespoon wine
1/2 teaspoon black pepper
2 tablespoons sesame oil

1 Set a steamer to boil.

2 Meanwhile, wash the tofu, drain well, and pat dry with paper towels (or let tofu drain on rack for a few hours before preparation). Use fingers to break up the tofu into a medium-sized heat-proof bowl.

3 Stir seasoning into the mashed tofu. Add also the diced mushroom and wood ears as well as the minced ingredients. Stir until evenly blended

4 Set the bowl of tofu mixture on a rack, cover steamer tightly with lid, and steam for 20 minutes. Remove from steamer, set the hot bowl onto a plate, and serve, garnished with chopped coriander.

Serves 4
Preparation time: **20 mins**
Cooking time: **25 mins**

'Numb Hot' Tofu

Ma la, 'numb hot', is the signature flavour of the Sichuan kitchen, and it goes very well with almost any sort of vegetarian dish that uses tofu. This highly aromatic, tongue tingling taste comes from the Sichuan peppercorn. It's a good idea to always keep a jar of freshly ground Sichuan pepper on hand in the kitchen, as well as on the table, either by itself or blended with ground sea salt.

2 tablespoons oil
3 slices ginger, minced
2 cloves garlic, minced
125 ml (1/2 cup) water
3 1/2 cakes firm tofu
    (about 400 g or 13 oz),
    cubed
160 g (1 cup) frozen
    mixed vegetables
    (peas, corn, carrots)
6 *shiitake* mushrooms,
    chopped
2 teaspoons ground
    Sichuan pepper
1 teaspoon ground black
    pepper
1 teaspoon cornflour
    mixed with 1 table-
    spoon water
1 spring onion (scallion),
    minced
1 fresh red chilli, finely
    sliced
1 teaspoon sesame oil

Sauce
3 teaspoons sweet
    hoisin sauce
1/2 teaspoon sugar
1 teaspoon soy sauce
2 teaspoons wine

1 In a bowl, stir together all the sauce ingredients and set aside.

2 Heat the oil in a wok until smoking hot, then add the minced ginger and garlic, and stir-fry 10 seconds.

3 Add the sauce, stir a few times, then add the water, and stir again to blend. When sauce bubbles to a boil, add the tofu, mixed vegetables and mushrooms and stir-fry to mix flavours. Cover, lower heat to medium, and simmer for 7 to 8 minutes.

4 Add the Sichuan and black peppers, stir to blend, cover, then let simmer 1 more minute before adding the cornflour mixture. Stir until gravy thickens then bring to the boil again.

5 Remove from heat, stir in the spring onion, chilli and sesame oil, and serve.

Serves 4
Preparation time: **5 mins**
Cooking time: **15 mins**

Tofu and Vegetables Stewed with Bamboo Shoots and Chinese Spices

This dish should be prepared in a heavy clay 'sand pot' (*sha guo*) cooker. If you cannot find one, then use a heavy 'Dutch oven' or slow cooker, which will do the job almost as well. The advantage of using a real traditional sandpot is that it is designed to allow all of the seasoning flavours to blend slowly and completely with the main ingredients; it also produces very tender texture and rich sauces.

1 litre (4 cups) water
2 20-cm (8-in) pieces dried *konbu* seaweed
2 teaspoons rice wine
1 cake soft tofu (about 300 g or 10 oz), cubed
1 medium white *daikon* radish, peeled, cut lengthways and sliced thinly at an angle
1 medium carrot, peeled, cut lengthways and sliced thinly at an angle
6 button mushrooms, wiped clean and cut into 3 pieces each
1 medium fresh or canned bamboo shoot, washed, drained and thinly sliced
2 medium white or yellow onions, peeled and cut into thin crescents
1 teaspoon sugar
2 teaspoons salt
2 teaspoons soy sauce
20 fresh snow peas, tops, tails and central rib removed
2 fresh red chillies, halved lengthways
3 teaspoons sesame oil

1 Put 1 litre water, *konbu* and rice wine into a clay pot cooker. Bring to the boil, then reduce heat, cover and simmer for 20 minutes.

2 Add the tofu, *daikon*, carrot, mushroom, bamboo shoot and onions. Stir in the sugar, salt and soy sauce, cover and simmer for another 10 minutes. Add the snow peas and chillies, simmer for 1 more minute, then turn off heat.

3 Drizzle in the sesame oil, stir to mix, then transfer cooker to the table and serve.

If you like chilli, you may add either a spoon of chilli sauce or a fresh red chilli cut in half lengthways to the pot along with the other seasonings. You may also mix and match various different vegetables, such as zucchini (courgette), yellow squash, cauliflower, and so forth. The sandpot cooker drives the flavours into whatever ingredients you put into the pot.

Serves 4
Preparation time: **30 mins**
Cooking time: **45 mins**

Stir-fried Tofu and Roasted Peanuts

This is a tasty, lively dish with firm and crunchy textures and plenty of spice. It goes well with rice, and could also be used as a stuffing for various wraps, such as Chinese pancakes, seaweed sheets, or whole leaves of iceberg lettuce. Chinese medicine lists the peanut as a highly nutritious food item that has particular benefits for the spleen and lungs. When purchasing roasted peanuts in the market, be sure that they have not gone rancid, and try to buy them roasted in the shell.

2 tablespoons cooking oil
2 fresh red chillies, halved, seeded and finely diced
3 cloves garlic, finely diced
2 slices ginger, finely diced
1 spring onion (scallion), finely diced
1/2 head round white cabbage, cut into 2-cm (3/4-in) squares
2 cakes dried tofu, cubed (to yield 3 cups)
65 g (1/3 cup) roasted peanuts, shells and membranes removed
1 small stalk fresh celery, tough fibres removed, finely diced

Sauce
2 tablespoons fermented hot bean sauce (*dou ban jiang*)
1 teaspoon sugar
2 teaspoons wine
1 tablespoon water

1 In a small bowl, stir all the sauce ingredients together and set aside.

2 Heat the oil in a wok until smoking hot, then fry the diced chopped chillies, garlic, ginger, and spring onion, then add the chopped cabbage and diced tofu. Stir-fry quickly for 1 minute.

3 Add the sauce, and continue to cook for about 4 to 5 minutes.

4 Add the peanuts, stir-fry another 30 seconds more or until peanuts are heated through, then turn off heat and transfer to platter. Garnish with the chopped celery and serve.

Instead of cabbage, you may substitute pickled bamboo shoots, finely chopped, for a different taste and texture. A dusting of Sichuan pepper-salt goes very well on this dish, for those who like the ma-la ('numb hot') taste sensation.

Serves 4
Preparation time: **20 mins**
Cooking time: **10 mins**

Golden Lily, Bamboo Pith and Wolfberry Soup

This is a soothing soup with cooling, calming medicinal properties. Its Chinese name translates as 'forget your troubles' and is derived from the combined effects of the tiger lily, bamboo pith and wolfberry, which calm 'liver fire' and relax the nervous system. Chinese vegetarian cuisine has a long tradition of blending beneficial medicinal herbs with ordinary food items to create dishes that nourish the body, correct imbalances and please the palate, all in one dish.

800 ml (3 1/4 cups) vegetarian soup stock, or plain water
1/2 teaspoon salt
1 tablespoon Chinese wolfberry (L. *Lycium chinensis*, see note)
50 g (1/2 cup) dried tiger lily buds (golden needles), tough bases removed, soaked 20 minutes and drained
6 pieces black wood ear fungus (or the equivalent dried; reconstituted in water for 20 minutes), cut into finger-thick strips
8 pieces dried bamboo pith, soaked in cool water for 20 minutes and snipped into 4-cm (3/4-in) lengths

1 Bring the stock or water to the boil with the salt, then add the wolfberry, and let water return to the boil. Add the flowers, wood ears and pith. Bring soup to a full boil, cover, lower heat, and simmer for 3 minutes.
2 Taste, adjust seasoning, then transfer to soup tureen and serve.

Chinese wolfberry, also known as Chinese boxthorn and matrimony vine, is available from Chinese medicine shops. For soups like this, it's a good idea to provide a tray of seasonings and condiments on the table, so that each person may season their soup to their own personal tastes. Try all of some of the following choices: sesame oil, red chi/li oil, Sichuan peppercorn-salt powder, chopped fresh coriander (cilantro), chopped spring onion (scallion), chopped basil, chopped parsley.

Serves 4
Preparation time: **15 mins + 20 mins soaking time**
Cooking time: **20 mins**

Chinese Angel Hair, Green Pea and Tender Tofu Soup

Chinese angel hair, or black moss fungus, is known in China for its blood-building properties, and as a tonic food that turns grey hair black again. It's also a delicious food with a delicate herbal flavour and chewy texture. Here it's combined with tofu and green peas to make a tasty, nourishing soup that's easy to prepare.

1 litre (4 cups) vegetarian soup stock, or plain water

1/2 teaspoon salt

1 medium carrot, peeled and diced into 1/2-cm (1/4-in) cubes

1 cake soft tofu (about 200 g or 6 1/2 oz), cut into 1/2-cm (1/4-in) cubes

80 g (1/2 cup) fresh or frozen green peas

1 handful dried black moss fungus, washed and soaked 10 minutes in cool water

3 teaspoons cornflour dissolved in 3 table-spoons cool water

2 teaspoons sesame oil

2 spring onions (scallions), chopped, to garnish

1 Bring the stock or water to a full boil with the salt, then add the diced carrot and tofu, cover, reduce heat to medium, and simmer for 3 minutes.

2 Add the green peas and fungus to the soup, cover and simmer for a further 2 minutes.

3 Stir the cornflour mixture into the soup. The soup will thicken as it returns to the boil. Drizzle in the sesame oil, add the spring onions, stir and turn off heat. Ladle into individual bowls and serve.

This soup goes well with a dash of ground black or Sichuan peppercorn. Another nice embellishment is to add a small handful of very fresh mung bean sprouts to each serving bowl before ladling in the soup; this adds both fresh flavour and a pleasant crunch to the texture.

Serves 4
Preparation time: 5 mins + 10 mins soaking time
Cooking time: 20 mins

Spinach, Mushroom and Tender Tofu Soup

1 tablespoon cooking oil
2 cloves garlic, smashed with side of cleaver, skin removed
2 slices ginger
300 g (10 oz) fresh Chinese spinach (*bayam*), washed and plucked
800 ml (3 1/4 cups) vegetable stock or plain water
1 cake soft tofu (200 g or 6 1/2 oz), cubed
1 cup canned button mushrooms, halved
2 teaspoons sesame oil
Salt and black pepper to taste

1 In a medium-sized saucepan, heat oil until smoking hot, then add the garlic and ginger and stir-fry quickly for 30 seconds. Add the Chinese spinach and stir-fry for about 2 minutes.
2 Add the vegetable stock (or water), tofu, button mushrooms and cover. Bring to a full boil, then lower heat and simmer for 2 to 3 minutes.
3 Turn off heat, stir in sesame oil and salt and pepper to taste, then transfer to soup tureen and serve.

If you prefer to eat this vegetable as a stir-fry rather than a soup, simply continue stir-frying it for another 1 to 2 minutes, and omit the soup stock and tofu. Sprinkle with deep-fried sliced onion, if desired.

Serves 4
Preparation time: **10 mins**
Cooking time: **10 mins**

Tiger Lily and Soy Bean Soup

1 1/2 litres (6 cups)
vegetable stock, or
plain water
100 g (1/2 cup) soy
beans, picked through
for grit, rinsed and
soaked overnight, then
drained
50 g (1 2/3 oz) dried
tiger lily buds or
'golden needles' (*jin
zhen*), washed, tough
bases trimmed
6 Chinese red dates or
jujube (*hong zao*),
washed, pits removed
2 slices ginger
Salt to taste

1 Bring stock or water to a full boil in a large pot, then add soy beans. Return to the boil, then cover, lower heat, and simmer slowly for 1 hour.

2 Add tiger lily buds and red dates, bring the soup to the boil again and boil for 15 minutes.

3 Add salt to taste, then transfer to soup tureen, garnish with fresh coriander, and serve.

At the end of the meal, there will be some soy beans remaining in the bottom of the tureen. Don't discard these. Instead, drain them from the soup, then heat 1 tablespoon oil in a wok to medium hot, throw in the cooked soy beans, 1 teaspoon sugar and 1 tablespoon soy sauce, and stir-fry for 1 to 2 minutes. This makes a delicious late-night snack!

Serves 4
Preparation time: **10 mins + overnight soaking**
Cooking time: **2 1/4 hours**

Stir-Fried Vegetables with Rice Vermicelli

This is a very quick and simple dish to prepare, perfect for preparing a fast lunch for a large number of people. Rice vermicelli is a popular alternative to wheat noodles in vegetarian cooking, and is an excellent choice for those who do not tolerate wheat products well.

1 teaspoon salt
200 g (6 1/2 oz) dried rice vermicelli
1 tablespoon sesame oil
2 tablespoons oil
1 cm (1/2 in) fresh ginger, finely shredded
2 cloves garlic, finely minced
6 large dried *shiitake* mushrooms, soaked in hot water 20 minutes, stems removed and sliced, reserve soaking liquid
1 teaspoon soy sauce
1 teaspoon sugar
1/2 teaspoon salt
1/2 head round white cabbage, shredded
1 small carrot, shredded
1 bunch garlic chives, snipped into 4-cm (2-in) lengths
1 tablespoon mushroom oyster sauce
100 g (1 cup) fresh mung bean sprouts, washed and rootlets removed
1 teaspoon black pepper
1 red chilli, sliced, to garnish

1 Bring a pot of water to a full boil with 1 teaspoon of salt, then add the rice vermicelli. Leave in water exactly 3 minutes, then transfer to colander and drain. Place noodles in a roomy mixing bowl and drizzle over 1 tablespoon of sesame oil; toss to coat thoroughly then set aside.

2 Heat oil in a wok until smoking hot, then add the ginger, garlic, and *shiitake* and stir-fry 1 to 2 minutes. Add the soy sauce, sugar, and salt, stir quickly to mix.

3 Next add the cabbage and carrot and stir-fry for 2 to 3 minutes; then stir in 3 tablespoons of the reserved *shiitake* water and cook for 2 to 3 minutes more.

4 Add the garlic chives and oyster sauce and stir-fry for 2 minutes, then add the bean sprouts and stir-fry another 1 minute.

5 Add the black pepper, stir to distribute evenly, then turn off heat, and transfer vegetables to the prepared rice vermicelli. Toss to combine, garnish with sliced chilli, and serve.

If you cannot find garlic chives, you may substitute spring onions (scallions) or celery. Chopped coriander complements the flavours of this dish well.

Serves 4
Preparation time: **15 mins + 20 mins soaking time**
Cooking time: **30 mins**

Fragrant Noodles
with Chilli and Sesame Sauce

Here's another quick and easy noodle dish, with a strong dose of fragrance and spice to brighten up your taste buds. As with most noodle dishes, the ingredients are very flexible, and you may add and subtract items, and balance the flavours, to taste.

1 teaspoon salt
250 g (8 oz) dried wheat noodles, any variety
1 tablespoon sesame oil
2 small Chinese cucumbers, pith and seeds removed, sliced thinly lengthways, then into long, thin strips
1 green capsicum (bell pepper), seeds removed and sliced into thin slivers
1 handful fresh mung bean sprouts, blanched 20 seconds in boiling water
1 pickled bamboo shoot, blanched, sliced and cut into thin sticks
1 small white or yellow onion, halved and thinly sliced
2 tablespoons black sesame seeds, toasted

Sauce
2 teaspoons red chilli oil
2 tablespoons dark sesame paste (or tahini) blended with 2 tablespoons water
1 tablespoon sesame oil
2 teaspoons sugar
1 tablespoon vinegar
1 teaspoon salt

1 In a roomy mixing bowl, stir all the sauce ingredients together and blend until smooth. Set aside.
2 Bring a large pot of water to boil with 1 teaspoon salt, then cook the dried noodles. (Cooking time depends on the type of noodle; follow label directions.)
3 Drain the noodles, rinse under cool water and drain again well. Place noodles in a large bowl and drizzle over the sesame oil. Toss to coat evenly.
4 Add the vegetables to the sauce in the mixing bowl and toss to mix well with noodles.
5 Dish out onto a serving platter, or divide into individual portions in small bowls, then sprinkle the toasted black sesame seeds on top.

The cucumbers used here are the small, firm, dark green variety used in Chinese salads and other dishes, not the large watery type. If fresh bamboo shoots are available, you may use them instead of the pickled type for a fresher taste and crunchier texture; boil them first for about 1 hour before cutting.

Serves 4
Preparation time: **25 mins**
Cooking time: **20 mins**

Dry Noodles with Sesame and Garlic Dressing

This traditional and very tasty form of Chinese 'fast food' is quick and easy to prepare and much better for your health—and digestive system—than burgers and fries! You may apply the recipe to virtually any type of noodle, adjust the sauce to your own taste, and add whatever sort of vegetables you like best.

1 teaspoon salt
250 g (8 oz) dried wheat noodles (or spinach or egg noodles)
1 handful fresh mung bean sprouts, washed and drained
2 spring onions (scallions), finely minced
1 red capsicum (bell pepper), seeds removed and cut into fine strips

Dressing
2 tablespoons dark sesame paste (or tahini) blended with 3 teaspoons water
1 teaspoon vinegar
1/2 teaspoon salt
1 1/2 teaspoons sugar
1 teaspoon mushroom oyster sauce (*su hao you*)
1 teaspoon soy sauce
1 tablespoon oil (olive, sunflower, grapeseed, or other high-grade oil)
2 cloves garlic, finely minced

1 In a roomy mixing bowl, stir together the dressing ingredients, then add in the minced garlic.
2 Bring a large pot of water to a full boil with 1 teaspoon salt, then add the dried noodles; return to boil and simmer until cooked (cooking time depends on type of noodle; follow label directions).
3 Drain the noodles well, then add them to the sauce ingredients. Toss all together with the bean sprouts, spring onions, and capsicum, making sure the sauce is evenly distributed before serving in a large bowl or in individual portions.

Try different types of noodles for diffferent versions of this dish, including Italian spaghetti and angel hair noodles. You may also use fresh noodles, if available. It's a good idea to offer an assortment of condiments and garnishes on the table, like chopped fresh coriander (cilantro) or basil, chilli oil and Sichuan pepper.

Serves 4
Preparation time: **10 mins**
Cooking time: **8 mins**

Mixed Vegetables and Noodles in Broth

Chinese distinguish between two basic ways of preparing and eating noodles: *gan mien* (dry noodles, i.e. with sauce and other ingredients but no broth); and *tang mien* (soup noodles, i.e. with seasonings and other ingredients in a broth). Here's a classic version of the soup noodle way of preparation.

1 1/2 litres (6 cups) vegetable stock, or plain water

1 tablespoon Chinese wolfberry (L. *Lycium chinensis*, see note page 27)

3 large dried *shiitake* mushrooms, soaked in hot water 20 minutes, then halved, reserve soaking liquid

2 teaspoons salt

2 teaspoons soy sauce

1 teaspoon sugar

120 g (1 cup) fresh lotus root, thinly sliced

140 g (3/4 cup) pickled bamboo shoots, blanched 1 minute and drained, halved length-wise and thinly sliced

150 g (5 oz) dried wheat noodles, any variety

100 g (2 cups) *bok choy*

2 teaspoons sesame oil

1 Bring the vegetable stock or water to the boil in a large pot. Add wolfberry and *shiitake*, cover and let boil 1 to 2 minutes.

2 Season with the salt, soy sauce, and sugar, then add lotus root and bamboo shoot. Cover, lower heat and simmer slowly for 3 to 4 minutes; turn off heat and leave to sit covered.

3 Bring large pot of water to a full boil, then add the dried noodles and cook (cooking time depends on variety of noodles used; follow label directions). Remove noodles from water, drain in colander, then add to the soup pot together with the *bok choy*, bring the soup back to a boil, then turn off the heat again.

4 Stir in the sesame oil, and transfer to soup tureen, or ladle into individual serving bowls.

This recipe may also be prepared with rice or bean vermicelli. Simply follow the label directions for preparing the vermicelli, then add it to the soup. You may also use any assortment of vegetables you prefer when making this dish; indeed it's a good idea to try a slightly different combination each time. Garnish with shredded basil or fresh coriander (cilantro).

Serves 4
Preparation time: 10 mins + 20 mins soaking time
Cooking time: 40 mins

Silk Squash Stir-fried with Garlic

Silk squash has a rich sweet flavour and creamy viscous texture that makes it one of the stars of the Chinese vegetarian menu. Easy to digest and highly beneficial to the bowels, silk squash also has 'cooling' energy properties and acts as an expectorant and demulcent to the lungs.

1 tablespoon cooking oil

4 cloves garlic, smashed and peeled

3 slices ginger, shredded

2 medium silk squash (angled luffa) (850 g or 1 3/4 lb), peeled, cut in half lengthwise, then sliced into 1-cm (1/2-in) slices at an angle (to yield about 3 cups)

1 teaspoon cornstarch dissolved in 2 tablespoons water

2 spring onions (scallions), cut into 2-cm (5-in) lengths, to garnish

1 red chilli, sliced, to garnish

Sauce

2 squares Sichuan fermented beancurd

1/2 teaspoon salt

1 teaspoon sugar

1 teaspoon sesame oil

60 ml (1/4 cup) water

1 Combine all the sauce ingredients, stirring to break up the beancurd, then set aside.

2 Heat the oil in a wok until smoking hot, then fry the smashed garlic cloves and ginger for 30 seconds.

3 Add the squash, stir-fry 1 to 2 minutes, then stir in the sauce. Cover, lower heat, and simmer until soft, about 4 to 5 minutes (check after 4 minutes, if all the water is evaporated, add a little more to prevent sticking).

4 Add cornstarch and water mixture to the squash, stir to incorporate, cover and simmer 1 more minute for cornstarch to thicken. Garnish with spring onion and chilli.

Serves 4
Preparation time: **10 mins**
Cooking time: **10 mins**

Spicy Spinach Stir-fried with White Fungus and Tofu Skin

This dish is packed with nutrients and medicinal elements, which make it an excellent dining choice for the ailing and elderly. White fungus has been renowned for centuries in China for its tonic benefits to the lungs and bowels, as a regulator of blood pressure, and a preventive for hardening of the arteries. Tofu skin provides abundant high quality vegetable protein, while spinach adds iron and beta-carotene.

2 tablespoons oil
2 cloves garlic, smashed and peeled
3 slices ginger
2 fresh red chillies, halved lengthwise, seeded, then halved again
1 medium white or yellow onion, halved, then cut in 1/2-cm (1/4-in) slices
2 clumps (1 cup) dried white fungus, soaked in cool water for 30 minutes, shredded (reserve 2 tablespoons of the soaking liquid)
2 sheets dried tofu skin, soaked in cool water for 20 minutes, sliced into strips 10 x 1 cm (4 x 1/3 in)
1 small carrot, peeled and thinly sliced
1 teaspoon sea salt
1 teaspoon raw sugar
1 teaspoon white rice vinegar
500 g (10 cups) spinach, rinsed well and cut into segments
1 teaspoon black pepper
2 teaspoons sesame oil

1 Heat the oil in a wok until smoking hot, then fry garlic, ginger, chillies and onion for 2 minutes. Add the fungus, tofu skin and carrot. Stir-fry for a further 1 to 2 minutes.

2 Stir in the sea salt, raw sugar, and the reserved 2 tablespoons fungus water. Cover with a lid, lower heat, and simmer for 6 minutes.

3 Add vinegar, stir to mix, then put in the spinach, black pepper and sesame oil and stir fry for another 3 minutes or until spinach is wilted and the stalks cooked through. Serve.

In this recipe, we specify 'sea salt' and 'raw sugar' for their superior health benefits compared with ordinary refined salt and refined sugar. In fact, if you are concerned about your health, you should always use sea salt and raw sugar in the kitchen, rather than the refined variety. If bamboo shoots are available, they make an excellent addition to this dish. Slice thinly, then cut into fine strips and add along with the tofu skin and fungus.

Serves 4
Preparation time: **20 mins + 30 mins soaking time**
Cooking time: **15 mins**

Broccoli and Cauliflower Stir-fried with Dried Mushrooms

Broccoli ('green flower vegetable') and cauliflower ('white flower vegetable') make an attractive couple in Chinese vegetarian stir-fry cookery, especially when accompanied by chewy *shiitake* mushrooms, whose texture, taste and colour nicely complement the crunchy vegetables. Broccoli and cauliflower have also been proven to contain potent antioxidant and cancer-preventive properties, and these are further amplified by *shiitake*. These therapeutic benefits are preserved by the Chinese method of cooking, which minimizes the exposure time to heat.

1 medium head broccoli, cut into florets
1 medium head cauliflower, cut into florets
85 ml (1/3 cup) cooking oil
4 slices ginger, thinly shredded
1 clove garlic, peeled and thinly sliced
2 spring onions (scallions), cut into 4-cm (1 3/4-in) lengths
6 large dried *shiitake* mushrooms, soaked in hot water 20 minutes, sliced into thin strips, (reserve soaking water)
1 tablespoon rice wine
2 teaspoons soy sauce
1 teaspoon salt
1 teaspoon sugar
2 teaspoons sesame oil

1 Bring a large pot of water to the boil. Put in the broccoli and cauliflower florets and let the water return to a full boil. Cook the vegetables for 1 minute, then drain into colander placed in a basin of cool, clean water. Set aside to drain.

2 Heat oil in wok until smoking hot; add the ginger, garlic, spring onion and mushroom. Then add the wine and soy sauce, and stir-fry quickly for 2 minutes.

3 Stir in the the caulifower and broccoli, then season with salt, sugar, sesame oil, and 1 tablespoon of the mushroom soaking water. Cook for 2 more minutes and serve.

You may substitute dried or fresh black fungus for the dried shiitake, *if you prefer, and you may also use any variety of fresh mushroom. Proceed exactly as above, but if using fresh mushroom or fungus, simply substitute 1 tablespoon of plain water for the mushroom water.*

Serves 4
Preparation time: **20 mins + 20 mins soaking time**
Cooking time: **15 mins**

Stir-fried Green Beans with Mung Bean Sprouts and Fresh Chillies

This dish is a power-pack of nutrients and therapeutic elements, combining the high vitamin and mineral content of green beans and chillies with the protein and enzymes of fresh bean sprouts, in a dish that is both attractive and delicious to eat. This combination is also very beneficial to digestion.

2 tablespoons oil
1 medium white or yellow onion, halved then thinly sliced
2 cloves garlic, chopped
300 g (3 1/2 cups) French beans (string beans), tops and tails removed, cut into 3-cm (1 1/4-in) lengths
2 slices ginger, thinly shredded
3 large fresh red chillies, halved lengthwise, seeded then cut into thin strips
1 teaspoon salt
1 teaspoon soy sauce
1 tablespoon rice wine
200 g (2 cups) fresh mung bean sprouts
2 teaspoon white vinegar
2 teaspoon sesame oil

1 Heat the oil in a wok until smoking hot and quickly stir fry the onion, garlic, French beans, ginger, and chillies for 30 seconds. Immediately add the salt, soy sauce and wine and fry for another 4 to 5 minutes.
2 Add the bean sprouts and stir-fry 1 minute, then add the vinegar and cook another 30 seconds.
3 Finally, add the sesame oil, stir to mix, turn off the heat, and transfer to platter and garnish with Chinese parsley.

You may also use soy bean sprouts, or any other type of fresh bean sprouts, to prepare this dish. If you like your chilli dishes fiery hot, retain the seeds and fibres in the chillies, or scrape away only half of them.

Serves 4
Preparation time: **20 mins**
Cooking time: **15 mins**

Kangkong Stir-fried with Fermented Black Beans

A rich source of vitamins B and C, water convolvulus, known locally as *kangkong*, is also a popular folk remedy for high blood pressure and fluid retention. Here it is stir-fried with fermented black beans, which assist digestion, strengthen the kidneys and build strong blood. Garlic adds both therapeutic potency and rich flavour to the dish. This combination has been a favourite in homes throughout China for many centuries, but is not often served in restaurants.

2 tablespoons cooking oil
3 cloves garlic, smashed and peeled, roughly chopped
1 tablespoon fermented black bean paste (see note)
600 g (1 1/3 lb) fresh *kangkong* (water convolvulus), snipped into 4–5 sections
2 red chillies, sliced

1 Heat oil in a wok until smoking hot, then quickly fry the garlic and black bean paste to release aromas, about 30 seconds.
2 Add *kangkong* and red chilli, lower heat to medium, and stir-fry continuously for about 3 minutes, or until wilted and the bean paste is evenly distributed.
3 Transfer to platter and serve immediately.

A type of fermented black bean paste with chilli may also be used in this dish. Also, ensure the kangkong *is completely drained before cooking.*

Serves 4
Preparation time: **8 mins**
Cooking time: **10 mins**

Tomatoes Stir-fried with Onions and Pine Nuts

This is another popular country dish that rarely appears on restaurant menus. Onions are tonic to the blood and promote circulation, while tomatoes have recently been proven to contain potent antioxidant properties that protect the liver from damage. It's a simple combination with a delicious flavour and goes well with almost all other dishes.

2 tablespoons cooking oil
3 medium ripe red tomatoes, each cut into 6 wedges
1 medium white or yellow onion, cut into 1-cm (1/2-in) dice
2 spring onions (scallions), cut into 1-cm (1/2-in) lengths
50 g (1/3 cup) pine nuts, toasted
1/4 teaspoon salt
1 teaspoon sugar
1 teaspoon soy sauce
Fresh coriander (cilantro) leaves to garnish

1 Heat oil in a wok until smoking hot, then fry the onion and spring onions quickly to release aromas, about 30 seconds.
2 Add the tomatoes, pine nuts, salt, sugar and soy sauce, and stir-fry continuously for 1 to 2 minutes.
3 Transfer to plate and serve immediately.

Serves 4
Preparation time: **10 mins**
Cooking time: **5 mins**

Cold Cut Plate of Seaweed, Broccoli, Daikon and Dried Tofu

3 20-cm (8-in) strips dried *konbu* seaweed, soaked in cool water for 40 minutes, rinsed and drained
2 squares dried tofu
1 medium head broccoli, cut into florets
1 medium carrot, peeled and sliced
8 large *shiitake* mushrooms, soaked in hot water 30 minutes
1 medium daikon (large white radish), peeled and cubed
2 florets fresh tree ear fungus, washed and drained
1/2 head iceberg lettuce, separated into leaves
3-cm (1-in) whole chunk ginger, smashed
1 fresh chilli

Stock
1 litre (4 cups) water
1 tablespoon five spice powder
1 teaspoon salt
2 teaspoons sugar
2 tablespoons wine
85 ml (1/3 cup) soy sauce
1 litre (4 cups) water
1 fresh red chilli

1 To prepare the seaweed rolls, roll up each piece of reconstituted konbu to form a roll, then pierce through it with a toothpick to hold the rolls in place, set aside.

2 To prepare the stock for braising, bring 1 litre water to the boil in a large pot. Add the rest of the stock seasonings and return to the boil.

3 Gently add all the prepared braising ingredients, except for the broccoli, into the pot, cover and when it comes back to the boil, lower heat to a slow simmer and cook covered for 30 minutes. Stir gently once or twice to prevent sticking. Ten minutes before time, add the broccoli.

4 Meanwhile, line a serving dish with the lettuce leaves.

5 When done, transfer cooked ingredients to a colander and drain over a bowl to catch the sauce.

6 When cool enough to handle, cut the tofu squares, mushrooms, and tree ears into bite-sized pieces ; cut the carrot, daikon, and broccoli into bite-sized chunks; remove toothpicks from seaweed rolls and cut each roll into thin slices. Arrange all cut ingredients nicely on the lettuce-lined platter.

7 Combine the drained sauce from the colander into a small saucepan along with the remaining sauce from the pot, and reheat. Drizzle 2 tablespoons of the sauce evenly onto the cut ingredients and serve.

Serves 4
Preparation time: 20 mins + 40 mins soaking time
Cooking time: 1 hour 20 mins

Carrot, Radish and Mushroom Stir-fry

This tasty blend of vegetables, seasoned with fermented bean sauce and other Chinese spices, provides a wide range of nutrients and medicinal elements, and also provides a very attractive combination of colours and textures. It goes well with rice, and may also be used as a stuffing for various crêpes and pancakes, *nori* seaweed wraps, or fresh lettuce leaves.

1/3 cup (85 ml) cooking oil
1 medium carrot, peeled and finely shredded
1 medium white *daikon* radish), peeled and finely shredded
5 large *shiitake* mushrooms, soaked in hot water 30 minutes, thinly sliced
1 fresh leek, green top discarded, sliced into quarters lengthways then cut into 3-cm (1 1/4-in) lengths
1 1/2 tablespoons fermented bean sauce (*dou ban jiang*)
1 tablespoon wine
1 teaspoon sugar
1 bunch (2/3 cup) fresh *enoki* mushrooms, tough ends removed
2 tablespoons sesame oil
Fresh coriander (cilantro) leaves, finely chopped

1 Heat oil in a wok until smoking hot, then add the carrot, *daikon*, *shiitake*, and leek, stir-fry quickly for 1 minute, then season mixture with the bean sauce, wine and sugar. Lower heat to medium-high, and cook for about 4 to 5 minutes.

2 Add the *enoki* mushrooms, stir-fry 1 to 2 minutes more, then stir in the sesame oil and turn off heat. Transfer to platter, garnish with chopped coriander, and serve.

If you prefer, you may use any variety of fresh mushroom in place of the dried shiitake. *And if you like a hotter flavour, you may include a teaspoon of your favourite chilli paste in the sauce mix.*

Serves 4
Preparation time: **20 mins + 30 mins soaking time**
Cooking time: **10 mins**

Sweet Green Lentil Soup

This ancient Chinese sweet course is extremely easy to prepare, and like most enduring favourites, it has potent health benefits. Green lentils have a cooling effect on the system, which makes this a popular snack for relieving the oppressive heat of summer. It is equally tasty served hot or chilled.

75 g (1/3 cup) green lentils, picked through for grit, washed thoroughly and soaked overnight in cool water, drained
1 litre (4 cups) water
5 tablespoons raw sugar

1 Place the drained lentils in a pot with 1 litre of water and bring to a full boil. Reduce heat to medium–low and stir in sugar. Simmer another 45 minutes or until beans are broken and soft.
2 Taste the soup and adjust if necessary, then turn off heat and transfer to soup tureen, or ladle directly into individual bowls and serve.

If you prefer the soup chilled, let it cool after cooking, then put it in the refrigerator for a few hours prior to serving. Large quantities may be prepared in advance and kept for 4 to 5 days in the refrigerator; this makes a very refreshing and healthy summer snack. You may also flavour the soup to your taste by adding a cinnamon stick, split vanilla bean, nutmeg or other spices to the water.

Serves 4
Preparation time: **overnight soaking**
Cooking time: **10 mins**

Sweet Red Date, Lotus Seed and White Fungus Soup

This is both a popular Chinese dessert soup and a traditional Chinese herbal remedy for high blood pressure, arterioscelorsis, insomnia and immune deficiency. All of the ingredients are important items in the Chinese herbal pharmocopeia, and together they provide a potent tonic boost to the human energy system. This makes it a particularly good choice in the daily diet of the elderly and those recovering from illness or surgery. In addition, it's very delicious!

30 dried white lotus seeds, soaked in cool water overnight
12 Chinese red dates or jujube (*hong zao*), washed and pits removed
3 whole florets white fungus (white tree ears), soaked in cool water for 1 hour, drained, tough bases discarded, roughly shredded
1 1/2 litres (6 cups) water
75 g (1/2 cup) rock crystal sugar

1 Drain the lotus seeds and place in a large pot together with the red dates, white fungus and water.
2 Bring to a full boil, then sweeten with the rock sugar. Cover, then lower heat to low, and simmer for 1 hour.
3 Taste the soup for sweetness, and adjust if necessary. Transfer the soup to a tureen or ladle into individual serving bowls.

If you like, you may add a split vanilla bean to the soup for additional flavour, but do not add cinnamon or ginger, because they alter the therapeutic effects of the main ingredients. This soup should only be served hot; eating it cold counteracts the medicinal benefits.

Serves 4
Preparation time: **overnight soaking**
Cooking time: **1 1/2 hours**

Sweet Pumpkin and Lotus Seed Soup

Pumpkin is one of the few vegetables that tastes equally good prepared sweet or savoury, which makes it a popular choice for desserts in Chinese cuisine. Here it's combined with lotus seeds and thickened with powdered lotus root, both of which have tonic herbal benefits.

1/2 medium fresh pumpkin (500 g), peeled with seeds and fibre removed, cut into bite-sized chunks

20 dried white lotus seeds, soaked overnight in cool water and drained

75 g (1/2 cup) rock crystal sugar

2 tablespoons dried lotus root powder, dissolved in 125 ml (1/2 cup) cool water for 2 hours (alternatively, substitute with 1 tablespoon cornflour or water chestnut flour dissolved in 1 tablespoon water)

1 whole floret white fungus (white tree ears), soaked in cool water for 1 hour, drained, tough base discarded, roughly shredded

2 litres (8 cups) water

1 Put pumpkin and water in a large pot and bring to a full boil, then lower heat to medium.

2 Add the crumbled white fungus, lotus seeds and the rock sugar. Cover and return to boil, then lower heat again to low, and simmer for 50 minutes.

3 Give the lotus root water mixture a final stir, then add to the soup, stir for 1 minute, replace lid, and simmer for another 10 minutes.

4 Turn off the heat, transfer to soup tureen, or ladle into individual serving bowls.

For variation, you may add a cinnamon stick, split vanilla bean, or other aromatic spices to the soup while cooking. If you can afford the cost and like the taste, try using 2/3 cup of maple syrup for a sweetener in place of the rock sugar, or use 1/4 cup rock sugar and 1/3 cup maple syrup. This provides a superb flavour, and maple syrup is also a rich source of essential minerals and trace elements.

Serves 4
Preparation time: **10 mins + overnight soaking**
Cooking time: **1 1/2 hours**

Index